THE WONDERFUL WORLD OF WORDS

4

Admiral Adjective and King Noun

Dr Lubna Alsagoff

PhD (Stanford)

Marshall Cavendish
Children

Admiral Angus Antillius Adjective and King Norman Nautilus Noun were very good friends.

They played together.

They went for walks together.

They flew kites together.

They even went fishing together!

Admiral Adjective and King Noun had a favourite word game.

The king would call out a noun and the admiral would then shout out an adjective to describe it.

sky

c _ _ _ r

The sky is _____!

6

11

Can you help me tell you about Mrs Fox? Unscramble the adjectives that describe the nouns in the passage.

When Mrs Fox went hunting for food, her children hid in the _ _ _ _ krad and _ _ _ _ yocs den and waited for her.

Mrs Fox was a _ _ _ _ ogod mother. She made _ _ _ _ urse that no _ _ _ _ _ _ ygruhn lion would be able to find them.

Mrs Fox was a very _ _ _ _ _ _ rlceev fox. She always knew how to run away from danger. She had _ _ _ _ _ rphas eyes and even sharper ears.

Mrs Fox had a _ _ _ _ _ `n o g l` and
_ _ _ _ _ _ `y u b s h` tail. It helped her run
very fast.

Mrs Fox lived in a _ _ _ _ _ `r w m a` den.
It was a _ _ _ _ _ `p d e e` hole in the ground
to keep her and her _ _ _ _ _ _ `t i l l e t`
foxes _ _ _ _ _ `e a f s`.

There, the _ _ _ _ _ _ `g u n o y` foxes
snuggled and slept soundly even when the wind
was very _ _ _ _ _ `c d l o`.

This is a red flower.

This flower is red.

Did you notice where adjectives are in a sentence? They always go with nouns.

My ship is magnificent.

I have a _____ _____ .

This anchor is rusty.

This ship has a _____ _____ .

The queen's crown is golden.

The queen wears a

_____ _____ .

The queen's car is shiny and new!

The queen has a _____ and _____ _____.

17

Giraffe is missing _____ at the end of his verbs!

Can you help Giraffe and Donkey say the sentences in the right way? Circle the words that are wrong and write them the right way.

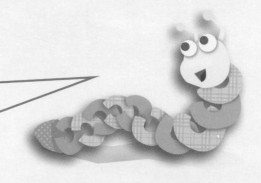

I am not feel well.

Me too. Head my is hurting.

Yesterday, I **walk** for many hours to get here!

I was so happy when I **reach** the clinic.

Owl has **help** so many animals. I hope it will be my turn soon.

Can you tell what's wrong with Boar?

Boar is missing _____ at the end of his verbs!

Dear Parents,

In this issue, children should notice and learn:

- how adjectives are used with nouns in two different ways.

- that word-endings like *ing* and *ed* are very important to verbs.

Page	Possible Answers
4-5	clear (sky) | blue (water) | bright (sun)
6-7	sharp (thorns) | heavy (anchor) deep (river) | fast (ship)
8-9	beautiful (flower) | purple (flower) huge (fish) | scary (fish) fast (fox) | quick (fox) tall (tree) | gigantic (tree)
10	small | big hot | warm
11	yellow | blue fast | slow
12-13	dark | cosy good | sure | hungry clever | sharp long | bushy warm | deep | little | safe young | cold
14-15	magnificent ship rusty anchor golden crown shiny | new car
19	Giraffe is missing *ing* at the end of his verbs!
20-21	I am not feeling well. My head is hurting. I hope that Owl is helping you. I have been practising my sentences. I keep practising, but I don't seem to be doing it right!
23	Boar is missing *ed* at the end of his verbs!